Best wishes,
Alexander Velky
17/11/15
x

"They thought we were using our money to make a statement about art, and really what we were doing was using our art to make a statement about money."   BILL DRUMMOND, *1997*

"Art is what is bought as art ... What defines art is therefore the act of buying something as art."   DAMIEN HIRST,* *2011*

*The unknown Slovenian artist Damien Hirst; not to be confused with the British artist of the same name.

MISTAKEN

ALEXANDER VELKY

FOR ART

HAS DOUBTS: VOLUME ONE

OR RUBBISH

dOUBTIST

DOUBTIST

Published by Doubtist Books, 2013

Doubtist Books
Tynewydd
Walton East
Clarbeston Road
Pembrokeshire
Wales
SA63 4TA

doubtistbooks@gmail.com
www.doubtist.com

© Alexander Velky, 2013

All rights reserved. No part of this publication may be reproduced in any manner, for any purpose - except brief excerpts for reviews - without the prior written permission of the author.

ISBN: 978-1-909812-00-0

Design: Zef Cherry-Kynaston

For VICTORIA *and* SYBIL

ACKNOWLEDGEMENTS

Thanks to Rennie Sparks of The Handsome Family for allowing a few lines from the song Amelia Earhart Vs. the Dancing Bear from the band's 1996 album Milk and Scissors to be misquoted herein. And thanks to the Slovenian Damien Hirst for giving me the permission to use some of his words to help introduce this volume.

Thanks also to Bill Drummond, Nina Persson, Pierre Pinoncelli, Pablo Picasso, Chumbawamba, Aleister Crowley and anybody else living or dead who I've quoted or misquoted, knowingly or unknowingly, without consent.

Thanks to everyone who pledged money and placed orders via Kickstarter. Thanks to Karen Kynaston for providing the cover photograph and for help with funding the collection, to David Nixon and Adam Haslewood for their help with the editing, and to Zef Cherry-Kynaston for his invaluable and sympathetic efforts on the design and typesetting.

Earlier drafts of most of these poems were once published on my blog. Thanks to those who noticed.

CONTENTS

1. Please don't fund my art 12
2. Alchemy 14
3. A duck with two heads 16
4. Poems about nothing 18
5. An interest in cartography 20
6. Martin Brady likes your link 24
7. The art factory 26
8. My art is greater than your art 28
9. Top ten indefinities ever 30
10. Your Nazi tattoo 34
11. A verse for the averse 36

12. Damien Hirst responds to his critics 38
13. Lost object 40
14. Doubts 42
15. "Celebration Mix" 46
16. Sonnets for plop 48
17. Art school 50
18. Money to burn 52
19. How to decide whether something is art 54
20. Cost 56
21. Poverty 58
22. All that is free 60

23. The box 62
24. Torture porn 64
25. Dead by Christmas 66
26. Klára 68
27. Destroy your art 72
28. Ill of the dead 74
29. Economics 76
30. The crowning 78
31. Sculptures of nothing 80
32. Doubtless 84
33. Mistaken for art or rubbish 86

NB – please read the poems in the above order, from start to finish.

Please don't fund my art

Benefactress, retired actress,
Please don't fund my art.
Upper crust, Prince's Trust,
Please don't fund my art.

I've a pen and I've a pencil,
I've some spray-paint and a stencil;
Arts Council England, would you
Please not fund my art?

Family, friends, dividends,
Please don't fund my art.
Perishing uncle in New Zealand,
Please don't fund my art.

I'd hate to owe you any fealty
For my food or for my realty,
Poetry Book Society, would you
Please not fund my art?

Highland Toffee, Costa Coffee,
Please don't fund my art.
Transport for London,
Please don't fund my art.

I've no harness for my hobby,
I've no beat and I've no bobby,
Deborah Meaden, would you
Please not fund my art?

Alchemy

I have mastered the equation,
Discovered the coveted deed,
Unlocked the fabled formula,
Now, you poets all take heed;

Once I plied my trade in silence,
Now I publicize my plight:
Spill my guts upon these pages
Once so wonderfully white,

Then announce myself from stages –
Hark, the herald: he so bold;
I have perfected the process
Of turning poetry into gold.

But now there's something niggling,
Some itch I can't quite scratch;
I've got the finest fountain pens
But I want my poetry back.

I've sung the praises of a leader
On a coronation day;
I said everything they wanted
Then had nothing left to say.

I've heard my stanzas sung by choirs,
Seen them written six feet tall,
Had quotations from my verses
Chiselled into city walls;

I only wear the finest tailored suits
Of the most fashionable cut,
I've a really rather lovely waistcoat
That conceals my newfound gut,

I quit my dayjob at the drop
Of somebody else's hat,
I got a desk and a business card
With a registered trademarked splat.

Now I miss the surreptitiousness
Of writing on the train,
Or at my laptop on my lunchbreak
Squeezing phrases from my brain.

I turned my reams of seamless verses
Into something white and black;
It's been mass produced and distributed
Now I want it back,

Once I flirted with an artist
Now I wake up with a hack
I don't recognize my reflection
Now, I want the poet back.

I had jewels and precious metals
Delivered to me in a sack
I have spent till it's half-empty
Now I want my poetry back.

Once I started a rebellion,
Then I signed a quick contract,
Now I have to start rebellions
And I want my poetry back.

I turned my idle musings
Into something that could be sold
And I want bodily fluids,
Not this metal, hard and cold;

But it's a chemical reaction,
Science says there's no reversal.
Simon says "Bend over, baby,
This is not the dress rehearsal;

"You've sold your soul for success,
So sucking will soon be second nature;
You'll find your rhymes unwinding
Now those loans have come to mature."

A duck with two heads

I've passed through the rapids
On a duck with two heads,
Now I'm buggered if I'll get out of bed

For a knock on the door
By a man with no ears
Who is begging in French to be fed.

I've defused explosive
Devices in crises,
As smoke spread and pillars crashed to the ground,

Now I won't step aside
For a man half as wide
As the ego to which he is bound.

I've invented ideas
But now I'm in arrears
For I've lent my soul to circumspection,

And that duck with two heads
Has come back for his bread;
In his four eyes I see my own reflection.

And I don't look too clever
And I don't look too sure
About the balance between knowledge and joy;

His beaks are both barbed and
His four eyes look half-starved
And he remembers what I promised him

When
I
Was
A
Boy.

There's a man digging for lugworms –
Or scallops, or razor clams, or something –
Out in Holes Bay when I get home
Almost every day:

Depending on the turn of the tide,
And whether or not I've been to Asda
And waited in the self-service checkout queue,
Watching imbeciles argue with robots
As the sun goes down outside.

Sometimes he's two men;
On the weekend once he was three,
But, either way, there he is
With what I assume is a spade

And what can only be a bucket
By his side, and a trail of upset mud
In his wake – as if life wasn't hard enough
For mud, these days.

I watch him sometimes –
Sometimes when I'm supposed to be
Doing something else –
And think "There's a poem in that,
Somewhere: but I don't know what it is."

No doubt it would be a better one
If I were doing the digging,
But look at me – I'm not about to
Get up to my knees in mud for
Some spineless hors d'œuvres.

Not at this time of year.
I've got better things to do,

And it looks cold out there,
And my laptop light's enticing,
And I've got better things to do
Like writing poems
About nothing.

Poems about nothing

An interest in cartography

When I was young I conquered all that I surveyed:
Climbed cliffs in school shoes,
Dug pits with picks and spades
In the corners of the garden where it was allowed;
Shouted out loud what I liked and listened
As the wounded hillsides
Took split seconds to agree with me –
Seconding my sentiments
With seemingly sentient glee.

Have or have-not haversack,
I'd ramble, bramble, itch and scratch.

With my mapmaker's eye
I made mincemeat of the sky
And moulded clouds to suit my moods:
I'd play with clay and plaster;
Draw colours from the sunset
With the best of my tools;

Make fools of weather forecasters,
And clasp cold breezes to my chest;
Braving thunder, lightning, rain,
I'd come home wet-through and full of wonder;
Investing my ambition in a golden net,
In which to catch words,
With which to build a model village of my world.

What happened to that plan?
I half forget.

But I unfurled my failures as sails
And crossed oceans of opportunity –
Still as mill-ponds –
Rowing, always rowing;
Showing no signs of flagging
Beneath ever changing colours.

Full of failure, primed with pride;
Fixed to take a lion-tamer for a bride,
And to woo her with my wounded paws
Upon her knees, if she should please
To pick the pricking thorns from out my side.

I'm no great cook; could I be Scott?
Or am I just a lost and lowly sot
Without a jot of jotted lines and dots
To impress me as a forget-me-not?

I was a bored explorer when I found you:
An amateur cartographer
With a shaky hand and blurred vision.
I tried to scale your face,
But my placement lacked precision;
I was snow-blind to your behind;
Mistook your skin, at times, for mine;
Heeded nary a warning sign;
Did my level best not to depress, but to impress;
Confused your mountains, once, with breasts.

I stood and waited by a frozen lake,
Making out mirage mistakes,
Blanketed in yesteryear's pelt,

Trying to focus on feelings felt,
Waiting for the footprints I saw
To either thaw and melt or fill:
These paths to overgrow,
These ill inklings to kill.

I hear you say
"If you want me, I'm your country."

But every ashen emperor
Is forever saying sorry.

Am I a Roman?
Abusing and confusing an existing infrastructure?
Am I the quarryman? Are you the quarry?
If I straighten the communications
Between your axes and projections
Will I be able, then, to navigate
The surface of your skin in straight directions?
In the pools that fools call eyes,
Will I see my own reflections?

Are you now my land?
Could I raise my flag on you?
Or are you always someone else's country?
Am I only passing through?
Am I Gypsy, or a Jew?

Am I making light of you?

Can I do right by you?

I'd like to be complicit in your upkeep –
Patrol your borders, see your sights –
Because you keep me up all night
Even when your lights are out,
Or when they're on but no one's home;
When your sacred rivers have run dry,
Or your pleasure domes are overgrown.
I'd like to feel if there's some upset
To your environmental make-up,
That it's partly down to my faults
And I'm due some kind of shake-up.

And I'm learning all your ways,
And your many moods amaze me.

I try not to let it faze me,
But I know I've got so far to go.

When you breathe a certain way
You blow me away.
When you laugh your loudest
You shake me to my bones.
When I miss you –
When I cannot kiss you,
When you block the signal on my phone –
You're as here and gone as a midnight train.
When you cry you're a monsoon,
And when the rains have come and gone
Sometimes the floods remain
(On the plane, in the main)
And a rot sets in to everything,
And I fear what was further than far
Has now come near.

When I lament the many eyes –
Some perhaps less green than mine –
That wondered at your landscape,
Ventured through its scenes sublime,
Before our climates climbed together,
And our twin breaths intertwined;
When I curse the tardiness that echoes
In my expedition's every hollow rhyme,
I can only bring to mind –
Can just remind myself a second time –
That only measurements exist in time:
Not moments, momentous or otherwise;
Not flutters of the heart
Or hard-luck lullabies;
Only arrivals and departures –
Be they early, be they late;
Only numbers, units, digits, dates;
Not the irregular contractions of
A muscle pumping blood;
Only grudges, greed and graves –
Not love.

Martin Brady likes your link

for MARTIN BRADY

The internet's an empty space,
Like any city marketplace
You care to stalk on Sunday, lone,
With saliently silent phone;

Where gazes meet but do not greet,
But glaze, continue on their beat;
Where screams can sound like muffled sighs,
And every breath, once birthed, soon dies.

I am not stupid: though it seems
The size of all my soundest schemes
Amounts to no more than hoping
That some publisher is scoping

Every last dire poetry blog
That willowisps through digifog,
I'm resigned to obscurity.
Not without insecurity;

I'd like data to bait critics
When I check my analytics;
Approval, however disparate,
Helps me feel that bit less desperate.

Once I've poured my heart out neatly
Into a template – discreetly
Spellchecked by some robotic ghost –
And swallowed once and then pressed "post",

The lengthy silence following –
As lengthy as a piece of string –
Recreates that queer sensation:
Dreams spent naked at bus stations.

I am inspired by simple things:
The joy a well-made cuppa brings;
The flight of birds, the sound of trains;
The smell of pavements when it rains.

I don't ask much and life replies
With frequent shrugs and rolls of eyes;
So when I lose my meanings thus –
So many badgers, so much bus –

Sighing, gathering my jacket;
Just when I feel I can't hack it,
"Ah! Things aren't so bad," I think:
"Martin Brady likes my link."

The art factory

There's an industrial hum
At the art factory.
You can feel how far we've come
At the art factory.
There's a production line
Where every organ beats in time
With the precision of a mime;
There's every flavour of chewing-gum,
And all three types of wine.
Thanks for asking, we're doing fine
At the art factory.

They used to make tinned soup
At the art factory,
But now we can another kind of gloop
At the art factory.
Life is bourgeois in the booth;
But there's a veil of sorts that lifts
When the gaffer whistles shifts,
And we pigeons fly the coop
To the coup d'état of youth,
From the cutting of a milky tooth,
From the art factory.

There's a momentary lapse
At the art factory
When the sunshine glints through gaps
At the art factory.
We see things in a new light:
These coloured dots we paint
Suddenly seem so frail and faint,
But the foremen in their flat-caps
Remind us that this isn't true light:
More a simply-will-not-do light
For the art factory.

A man once smelt a rat
In the art factory,
So the man spray-painted that
On the art factory.
Now that man works in the next booth
Painting rats on a cup and saucer.
On his lunch break he reads Chaucer,
Eats cakes that will make him fat,
And makes remarks markedly uncouth.
But people hate to hear the truth
At the art factory.

There is obsolescence inbuilt
At the art factory;
An unshakeable sense of guilt
At the art factory.
I am here for my career:
I keep my head down, do my job;
Pull this lever, turn that knob.
But when I cower beneath my quilt,
Sweating alcohol and fear,
I feel I'll never be far from near
To the art factory.

My art is greater than your art
Because it deals with pressing issues,
Yet remains aesthetically pleasing.
It can be framed and nailed to a wall,
Or hung by a hook from the ceiling.
My art is greater than your art
Because it describes how I'm feeling,
And I know you don't get it at all,
But you are not a god worth appeasing.
Yours is a machine, fit to disuse;
My art is greater than your art.

My blog is better than your blog:
Don't judge its comments, or lack thereof;
Read me and you're awed into silence.
I do not want a conversation;
I'm a rally, not a conference.
My blog is better than your blog
Because you're under the influence
Of Vice Bloggers' Network. Conflation
Of conflicting content breeds violence,
Leaves a mess. I digress: all three of
My blogs are better than your blog.

My brain is bigger than your brain:
It's grander than a grandfather clock;
It's learnt more than you'll ever forget,
Forgotten more than you'll ever learn.
Your cell's lonely, mine are all crowded;
My brain is bigger than your brain:
With mystery it is enshrouded;
I have got philosophies to burn,
In every idea I beget
Lurks revolution: a short, sharp shock.
My brain is bigger than your brain

And don't get me started on my cock.

My art is greater than your art

Top ten indefinities ever

At ten is the time a Coptic
Bishop tried to take a shrimp from
The grill at a church fundraiser
On the expansive lawn of the
Diocese of Melbourne HQ,
And he swore – till his pancreas
Succumbed to adenosquamous
Carcinomas – that it said, "Wait!
I am not yet sufficiently tender."

At nine is the time a young boy
Serving as a squire to a knight
Who claimed to be descended from
Sir Galahad saw in his shield –
While polishing it on the ninth
Hour of the ninth day of the ninth
Month of the Ninth Crusade – a cup
Of pure gold reflected in its
Old weathered face, radiating splendour.

At eight is the time a Russian
Painter, a short time after the
February revolution,
Succumbing to paraplegia,
Set out to paint a domovoi
Watching a merchant's wife sleeping,
And discovered with his last stroke
That he had no idea with whom
He identified most – her or the beast.

At seven is the time a wolf –
Lost at sea for seven long months
After a storm broke and the waves
Came down on the low coast in ways
They'd not before and haven't since –
Managed to swim back to her pack
And teach them the difference between
South and north, though she never grasped
The concept of a need for west or east.

At six is the time a sati
("A", not to be confused with "the")
Made a plea to the governor
Of the Tamil Nadu branch of
The East India Company
That went all the way up to the
Governor-General in Bengal,
And he put a stop to the whole
Self-immolation thing, a day too late.

At five it has to be the time
A Portuguese conquistador
Lost his bearings (and his llamas)
Looking for the Qulla Suyu,
Hoping they would help him locate
El Dorado (or Tuvalu,
Or his marbles, or his llamas);
He walked the Atacama sands
In circles till his curly hair grew straight.

At four is that weekend in Bath,
August, 1894, when
Thousands of jellyfish – about
The size of a shilling piece each –
Fell from the skies of Somerset
And one lady pushing a pram
All across the Royal Crescent
Ran right into the ha-ha and,
Though unhurt, never mentioned it in jest.

At number three with a bullet
(Because you must have heard of it)
Is the time a Jewish merchant
Lost a pound of flesh in Venice
Running from angry creditors,
Jumping crates and cutting corners;
Falling into a canal, he
Commandeered a gondolier –
Who later wed him, she was that impressed.

At two is the time a man was
Two-timing these two twin sisters –
"It's a win-win situation!"
He'd say to anyone who would
Listen – but he'd no notion of
The vagaries of double-crossed
Moroccan ladies; and the tricks
They turned against him in the end
Made him swear he'd never turn one again.

But, after all, the best is still
The time a tyrant with a quill
Decided to define the world
In terms that only he could learn,
And in the rarest molluscs' ink
He etched out shapes and named them words,
And told his slaves they couldn't sing
But instead must start compiling
Excuses for the funny ways of men.

You wear your sleeves long all the year round
To hide your Nazi tattoo,
Where the needle sank in to your shallow skin
Between veins of Prussian blue.
It's only one of eleven marks
That stain your Aryan hide
But it's come to be something of a barrier
Between you and those outside.

You remember why you paid for it
But you weren't the same man then;
And you've paid for it since, and I'm unconvinced
You won't pay for it again.
You cite your acquaintances' races;
Your wife – you say – is a Jew.
But they won't let you define it in that way;
They say that it defines you.

You know your rights, I know. And I know
You're right, and you know your wrongs.
Though you've never had much of a singing voice
I've often enjoyed your songs;
But, watching you sing, I'm wondering
Just how it feels to be you:
In the bath, bald, naked, overweight and old,
Washing your Nazi tattoo.

Your Nazi tattoo

A verse for the averse

for MARJORIE SPONHOLZ-TUTTLE

The muse, the muse who used to hue my blues,
The muse who used to choose my don'ts and dos,
Who used to find me the right words (and lose
The wrong ones) from my poems and my songs,
Has gone: has donned his or her shoes and split;
Has quit, has buggered off, and won't come back.

Alas, alack: lack of inspiration
Is all that follows my perspiration
Now; my pencils are blunt, my paper's blank,
And my back aches from hours hunched over black
Plastic keys with white capital letters.
I'm no better than the gaps between them,
Where dust collects and maybe mates with crumbs.

I succumb to something I've heard bemoaned:
Something – studies have shown – strikes artists down
Like a common fever, a snapped lever
On a runaway train, or a dry rot;
The writers like to call it "writer's block".
(Note the apostrophe – all me, me, me.)

I wonder what the painter calls it though.

Anyway: once upon some times like these
I'd sojourn mournfully and talk to trees,
Or else thumb through embarrassed diaries:
Try kissing back to life those younger mes.

But now – in my finite wisdom – I sigh,
Laboriously blink dry sleepless eyes,
And theorize my self-diagnosis:
Causes, symptoms, treatments and prognosis.
Could hypnotism help end this schism?

Who cares? I come over all laissez-faire:
No longer grind my teeth or tear my hair;
I stare dog-dumb at walls; dial old close-calls,
Ask questions I'm not sure I want answered
And find them all as useless as ever –
Whether more or less patient or clever.

One doesn't want to write for the needing:
Sometimes one doesn't need to write at all.
But mostly one can't write for the thinking:
Thinking one need cast light over it all.

I thought on till I'd tied my mind in knots.
I expected an answer. I found lots.

Now I amuse myself by searching for
The muse in me: try to inspire myself,
Because no one else will line my bookshelf
With what I could have written had I not
Been smitten by that concept called "the muse".

Though the world is filled with many fine feet –
Each prowling their own beat, completing feats –
No four are the same: none can fill my shoes.

Damien Hirst responds to his critics

for DAMIEN HIRST*

"You've backed me into a corner,"
I said, by way of trying to warn her.
I'm in talks with an oligarch:
We meet in Mayfair, after dark;
He says I'm the man to make him feel royal,
And that I am to art what he is to oil.

I never stole from John LeKay.
How do you define "stealing", anyway?
There's no shame in taking notions
And then giving them promotions.
Germaine Greer says my rationale's threadbare,
But my brand, even she concedes, is beyond compare.

* The unknown Slovenian artist Damien Hirst; not to be confused with the British artist of the same name.

They all cite the value of my art as a sum,
Therefore the art of value is what it's become.
Only by emptying the mind does the heart grow full:
Which one of you will buy my diamond skull?

The papers cry vulgarity:
They don't give me the slightest charity.
There's an African dictator
I'm meeting for coffee later:
He'll want to know the stones are ethically sourced;
He'll need to know that the message wasn't forced.

If I take money to death's door
Then what was all that dying even for?
There's no harm in taking payment
From a benefaction claimant.
Send the editors the news that 50 Cent
Is this close to putting down a downpayment.

I wanted to make something beautiful for once.
The production of this piece took me many months.
You can call me crass, but don't ever call me dull,
Because I made a diamond-studded human skull.

It struck me that the price of fifty million quid
Was too big a bargain for me to leave unbid.
I called a few friends and over it they did mull
Till they agreed to help me buy my diamond skull.

I found an object in a location.
So it became my property.
I attached to it a value,
And I discussed it over cakes and tea,
Over cakes and tea.

I have put it in a situation,
Removed its objectivity.
Now my object is a subject:
A testament to creativity,
Creativity.

Its absence causes them perspiration.
They pressure me to name its price.
They don't understand my object;
They'd have it washed and dried and smelling nice,
Dried and smelling nice.

My object's not for regeneration.
I have named it "Forget-me-not".
You can't pickle it in fluids.
You have to sit and wait and watch it rot,
Wait and watch it rot;

Watch it interact with its surroundings;
Watch its physical make-up change;
Watch your own delayed reactions
Reflect limited emotional range,
Emotional range.

I lost an object but found a subject.
I found a way to lose control.
I found a way to lose an audience.
Commission me, I'm on a roll,
Me, I'm on a roll.

Lost object

Doubts

I have my doubts.
I probably have some of yours;
So give me just a moment
While I impregnate this pause.
If you note some correspondence
Between my and your despondence
Maybe our mutual abscondence
Can make peace among these wars.

I have self-doubts;
I doubt my fears are as logical
As I'd like them to be.
I doubt if I really tried
I could not learn to ride a bike
Before it learned to ride me.
I doubt if I lied I could hide my deception
Sufficiently to avoid your detection.
I doubt I've the courage
Of all of my convictions;
I doubt I can maintain smooth-talk
In the face of friction.
I doubt my diction's as dictionaryesque
As it should be:
My definitions put to the test
Show there could be
Room for improvement;
I am not much for movement:
I doubt even if proven wrong I would be.

I sometimes whisper
When I ought to be screaming.
I sometimes dither
When I ought to be scheming.
Sometimes when I ought to
Just speak, I shout
But these are not foremost
Among my doubts.
I doubt there's a God,
Although, I don't know;
And I feel the burden of proof
Lies with me to convince myself
What I ought to believe,
Not with you to show me
On what basis lies your truth.

I doubt everyone's definitions
Of good and evil are the same.
I doubt anyone dares define them
Definitively, distinctively for infinity,
For fear of footing the blame.
I doubt anyone cares if they do or do not
Do it in my name.

I doubt my name – Alexander Velky.
I doubt if you don't understand it
Any amount of explaining will help me
Sell it to you. If I tell it to you true,
And don't excuse myself,
I might just lose myself –
Or worse, confuse myself
With somebody else.
Tell me, would that be healthy?

Besides, I doubt there's much in a name at all.
I doubt that the future can be written on a wall.
I doubt that pumpkin carriage will get me to the ball;
If it does I doubt that if I dance I will not trip and fall.
And then I doubt you will come out if I happen to call.

I doubt that you'd believe me if I said "I'm not a cynic"
But you ought to be able to see that with me
It's not what's in it but what's not in it,
And what's not in it is an answer
So I have to keep questing;
For unanswered questions
I'll keep putting my best in.

I'm a clinical believer
In the right to be wrong;
It's the philosophy I have so far
Maintained all along
And it's got me this far,
It's what it's all been about:
I've built a life of struggle, strife and striving
To defeat my doubt;

But I have my doubt to thank
For all that I hold dear in this world:
Every obstacle I've overcome,
And every sail unfurled;
Every target I hit,
And every goal that I score;
Every fact that I have factored,
Every thousandth metaphor;
Every word absurd that somehow seems
To help me make some sense
Of the planet I inhabit;
Each attack and each defence;
My assertions, my aspersions –
Circumlocution or clout;
It's all down to dedication
And my doubt,
Doubt,
Doubt.

"Celebration Mix"

for K'NAAN, *with sympathy*

War and famine won't sell soft drinks:
You can't be shoving that stuff down folks' throats.
Everybody loves football, though,
Even those with AKs in stolen boats
And we all drink Coke,
And we all drink Coke,

And pestilence and death don't mind
What our appetite for caffeine can't hide.
The wider audience knows that
International business trumps national pride
And we all drink Coke,
And we all drink Coke,

And we choke back the tears of joy
That artistic integrity can't buy.
Sing a song; sell a song: a dream.
Bring a smile: the truth just makes people cry.
And we all drink Coke,
And we all drink Coke,

And Chumbawamba once called this
"Coca-Colonisation" (with no zed)
But what do they know? Their World Cup
Song was shit; their career's as good as dead.
And we all drink Coke,
And we all drink Coke,

And
When you get older
Your nose grows harder;
You can see farther
Than the borders that fly your flag.

Oh, when you get older,
The winters get colder;
You can't warm your shoulders
With principles stitched to that rag.

Yeah, when you get older,
Survival guilt over:
You're jaded, persuaded
To finally furl that flag.

Because when you get older
You will be weaker;
To speak of the future,
You must forsake that flag.

Boy, when you get older
Your wounds last for longer,
Your enemies, stronger,
After they capture your flag.

Girl, when you get older
Your bugbears grow bolder,
Your blueprints fair moulder,
Your lackeys begin to lag.

Friend, when you get older,
Your plans come to flounder,
Your points become rounder,
The winds won't help wave your flag

And when you get older
Your heart beats hollower,
You'll be a follower,
And you will take down your flag.
Take down your flag.
Take down your flag.
Take down your flag.
Take down your
Flag.

Privacy is heresy nowadays.
The little things we once kept to ourselves –
In so many safes on so many shelves –
Would surprise us now in so many ways.
All the more reason to resent plonk and plop,
And the confrontation uninvited
From the artful conmen unindicted.
Could we but confine such stuff to a shop.
A shed once a boat now once more a shed
Is not a palindrome, and plinths are built
To boast glory – not shame, or blame, or guilt.
All that's required is a shake of the head:
"No, this tells me nothing about my kind."
We want reflection: like body, like mind.

Disgrace comes easy in a public place.
There are things we do when no one is near –
Out of sight of eye; out of shot of ear –
That would bring blood to the cheeks of each face,
And stop the pipes between lungs, tongue, and brain.
Actions, performed with or without a thought,
Could utterly trump any words you'd wrought
To weigh your transgression down to a plain
Idea; a societal mandate.
We've each and every one of us bought in,
So we really needn't put much thought in;
All we have to do is gesticulate,
State: "This doesn't speak to me about me;
Keep it to yourself." Like mind, like body.

Sonnets for plop

Art school

Welcome to art school,
Where we will teach you how to be cool,
How to disobey the rules,
And how to gladly suffer fools
Who rush into your dreadful dreams
And tread not softly on your schemes.

Welcome to art school,
Where you will learn where ideas come from
And how, if necessary, they can be run from
Or how you can try to stop the sun from
Shedding too much light on their naked flesh
Or bake tan lines onto them with mesh.

Welcome to art school,
Where you will be given the tools
To solidify tears and liquidize jewels,
To measure infinity in kilojoules,
And to bend and break the raw ingredients
Of unfounded objections into obedience.

Welcome to art school,
Where the greatest minds that ever thunk
Will impartially impart what's art, what's bunk;
Where you can drink in culture until you're drunk
And then vomit into your portfolio case,
Check your cache and fix your face.

Welcome to art school,
Where you will be groomed for an art career,
Where you will be taught to solidify a tear,
Where you will be encouraged to have an idea,
Where you will be forced to break a rule,
Where you will be qualified to be cool.

A sweaty grip on a suitcase handle,
The smoking wick of an altar candle,
Great expectations for a great escape,
A few reels of Hi-8 magnetic tape,
An empty boathouse somewhere on Jura:
An hour and seven minutes of torture.

An immolation to no deity:
No dance, no drink, no song, no gaiety;
An acrid smell and a sickening guilt;
The whole of the law being "Do what thou wilt",
Up the chimney with twenty thousand queens.
Salt on your eyebrows and ash on your jeans.

We love the taste of a courtroom drama,
Redistributing cultural karma:
The sanctity of sin without the taint.
We love the pictures we could never paint,
In well-lit spaces, neither hot nor cold,
Sponsored by petrol merchants, framed with gold,

But these mild, middle-aged men in the dock –
Who once were King Boy D and Rockman Rock –
Neither tries to protest his innocence,
Though they stand charged with the gravest offence:
Like Aleister Crowley and Oscar Wilde,
Their lives have become artworks much reviled.

That such a spectacle can soon wear thin
Is no testament to the time we're in,
It's more an awed discord with the weight
Of their material; we contemplate
Our lives, our deaths, the comparative worth
Of their work against any given birth.

We talk of madness, gluttony, and greed –
All concepts from which we'd gladly be freed –
But if you can't explain it to a child,
Is it complex, immoral, cruel or wild?
I think on this, and edge toward the fourth,
The JAMs on my headphones – *It's Grim Up North*.

Money to burn

Did genius effect its genesis?
Was it lovingly crafted by skilled hands?
Were its elements expertly blended?
Was it studied, intended, drafted, planned?
If it was not, it is not art;
Chit-litter has no place on my chart.

Does it command great material wealth?
Can its worth be weighed in heavy metal?
Will it mature like fine wine if cellared?
Has its status superpublicity?
If it has not, it is not art;
Just a cheap temptress: a pretentious tart.

Was it brought forth to this world in great pain?
Did its creator suffer for its birth?
Was hair tugged and torn to blasphemous words?
Do blood,tears and bile combine at its core?
If they do not, it is not art,
But a childish falsehood: false-hope, false-start.

Does it exist in a physical form?
Can you add depth to its two dimensions?
Can you play palps across its close contours
And, leaning in, inhale its history?
If you can not, it is not art;
Zeroes and ones do not beat this heart.

Is it composed, for the most part, from paint?
Is it, in fact, a painting on canvas
In oils distinct by blue and red tinctures
That one might describe as Pre-Raphaelite?
If it's not, I'll not call it art;
And in its patronage I'll play no part.

How to decide whether something is art

*C*ost

This poem is not worth
The paper it isn't written on,
Nor the face valuation of
The seat you're not even sitting on,
Nor your beating eardrums'
Holocausted calories;
No, not even the exhausted fumes
Of its multifarious similes.

This poem is not worthless
Because it could not be worth less
Than what it is worth,
Which is myrrh to the birthless,
Michael Buerk to the mirthless,
Bical to the Moët-mad heiress.
To say it's worth its weight in salt
Overstates its capacity to exalt.

This poem is a mistake,
I can tell that already;
I am not a visionary
For whom the world is as yet unready.
If anything, I am as Æthelred,
Readying myself to be unread;
Acting too late on ill advice:
Balls to the grindstone, axe in a vice.

This poem is priceless;
It's not to be sold separately
From the multipack from which
It is but profligate progeny.
To say its weight is measurable
Is to say that time is treasurable;
As much as man is malleable,
This poem can be called valuable.

This poem is not for sale.
If you paid for it with your broadband
Or the ill-gotten gains of your sword hand
You'll simply never understand
The true nature of sacrifice,
The price of a cost, the cost of a price,
The robbery of an unfair exchange,
The power of conformity to affect change.

Poverty

You are the crushed cans of Foster's
On the steps of Jobcentre Plus.
You're pornographic graffiti
On the back seats of the school bus.

You are the laminate flooring
Appliquéd to resemble pine.
You are the cigarettes I quit
So I could afford better wine.

You're the comfort of this metre,
The contraction that fits the bill,
The media through which my words
Must pass to cerebra from quill.

You are relativity itself;
You qualify all that is worth.
You are life expectancy,
And rate of survival in birth.

You are afternoons in Asda
When I'd rather be in Waitrose:
You are that inky cancerous
Cell that even the sultan knows.

You're aspiration's damnation:
The graveyard where hope's laid to rest.
At home as much in Abertawe
As you are atop Everest;

For you stalk Homo sapiens
From cradle to hospital bed,
And you care not for pentacles
Because you do not live on bread;

You thrive on fear and obedience,
And you feast on our apathy:
You're a weapon wielded by the few,
But they're tools to you, poverty,

Because they don't know how to be free of you:
They don't understand how you work;
They strive to shrug off your influence
With every chore that they shirk,

But all that they make of you that way
Is a black rod for their own bare backs;
And the longer the night through which they sleep soundly,
The longer the knives for their backs.

You're a culture that sells off its libraries
For a bucket to bail out its banks,
You're the message that learning's a luxury
Hung from the barrel of a tank;

But you won't have your way with us, this time,
Because we won't be left in the dark:
We have candles to hand out to the vandals
Who would sit and sing songs in the park

Warming their hands round the campfires
Built with the timbers of Rome;
For you may have a mortgage in Sandbanks,
But we call the whole world our home.

And you can't call us poor with a straight face
When the third world shifts closer by the day,
In spite of the spite of its tyrants
Who, like you, are poor in their own way.

And you can't stop us reaching our deities,
With your language of indecency,
And you can't put a price on our piety,
Because art is all that is free.

All that is free

"All that is free is careless," she said
"And all that is careless is false."
Those thirteen words went right to my head,
And beat through my sleep like a pulse.

I elected to do myself harm,
That I might then understand her:
Took a tool to my sinister arm,
Wrote there in blood "A L E X A N D E R".

From this prison I painted my pain
In acrylic primary hues.
I let my portrait run in the rain
While I was being sick in my shoes.

But who will buy my innocence lost?
Who will buy this experience?
Who will approximate that the cost
Is worthy of interference?

I will relinquish my grin, my groin;
I've played up my badly cast part.
Have them mint a commemorative coin
To be spent on state-funded art.

The box

Its dimensions are delicious:
All three of them equally so.
Its composition is comparable
In purity to snow.

Although it isn't uncomplicated;
It has a history
Of sorts. But details remain blurred:
Dates fast became a mystery

As wave upon wave of technology
Disappointingly lapped
Against its sturdy sides; and yet
Every time its flaps are unwrapped

Something stays locked inside.
I picked it up at a charity shop
In a cathedral city – I forget
Which one. I have to stop

Myself from speculating where
In the world it originates
From – that's not the point of it;
That just isn't how the box relates

To all that's within and without.
One night my cat got stuck in it.
At least, I think it did;
I thought it had, so I waited a bit

Before lifting the lid to see
If I was going mad. And now
I'm not entirely sure I ever
Had a cat. But that's just how

It works: sometimes it's a cuboid;
Sometimes it's a cube. Other times
It seems that no two sides are equal lengths.
It falls, sometimes; it climbs

As well. Once or twice it's reverted
To its plan. It ate a day
Last October, and threw it up,
Unprovoked, the following May.

I told it then to quit that stuff
Or I'd empty it out for good.
"You can't see the fin for the infinite,"
It said. But then, it would.

I wear the box as a hat sometimes
When no one else is around,
And smell its many soft smells
And listen to its many faint sounds,

But it hurts my head when I take it off:
Thinking becomes a chore.
I don't know then what to do with myself,
Or what I did before.

I told it once to pack its things and go:
I asked it what it brings.
"Don't judge a frame by its painting," it said.
It says a lot of things.

"Your dimensions are delicious:
All three of them equally so,"
I told it by way of a double-bluff.
The box just said: "I know."

Torture porn

Every generation gets the art it asks for.
Every epoch sports the culture it requires
To develop and disseminate its wisdom,
To advertise its fears and desires.
Every great leap forward in our understanding
Of equality and all that that should mean
Is tarred with the tallow from a history of harrowing,
And feathered with the repression of dreams.

I understand the value of shock tactics,
I appreciate the art of the outrage,
But the depths of depravity cut my teeth like a cavity,
Am I the Mary Whitehouse of my age?
In my opinion, Eli Roth is not an artist;
He's hardly even artful at his best.
All he does is rake subconscious silt and serve it back to you as guilt
I'd not urinate on flames at his behest:
I'd not urinate upon his flaming vest.

All he's done to fill the silence
Is to combine sex with violence:
It's no secret recipe, is this cocktail, oh, my boys;
It's no secret recipe, oh, my girls.
But the lovers and the haters and the messageboard masturbators,
Detractors and fanatics, all have sworn
That with his dreary Hostel, a new medium was born:
A medium they're calling "torture porn", oh my boys,
A medium they're calling "torture porn".

Does my plea for decency make me a deviant?
Does my requirement for some depth make me a prude?
If a film finds a home in our cinemas today,
Does it necessarily follow that it's good?
Can we be surprised by the success of this franchise,
Given the foundations on which it is built?
There's no better bedfellow, it seems, to lurid lusts and violent dreams
Than a vengeful God and good old Catholic guilt.

And you may very well protest your atheism,
Or whatever other faith you subscribe to,
But the hand of history holds you and its legacy enfolds you:
The bad bits of the Bible, they imbibe you, yes they do:
The good bits, yes, but the bad bits, they do too.

When Jehovah recommends rape as a weapon of holy war
You wonder whether feminism is even worth fighting for.
Isaiah, thirteen: fifteen to sixteen, oh my boys;
Isaiah, chapter thirteen, oh my girls.
But the idealists and dreamers and the anti-social schemers,
Feminazis, fools and faggots, all forlorn,
Will try to do away with torture porn, oh my boys,
They'll try to rob us of our torture porn.

Censorship's a sinking ship they tell me.
In the Free West even Fred Wests should be free
To publish and create things, film themselves masturbating:
Call it art, screen it and charge a fee (for entry),
Call it art, screen it and charge a fee.
As long as the Daily Mail can be outraged:
As long as they can clamour for a ban
Alongside all their own published sensationalist salaciousness
And articles about how immigrants raped your gran, raped your gran,
About how immigrants will definitely rape your gran.

I know it can sometimes seem funny
But bear in mind people pay money
To poison their brains with this heavy horse shit, my boys,
To poison their brains with this, oh my girls.
You can watch the squabbling of the right wing and the left wing,
Shake your head and wait for a mild morn:
But the grass will be soaked with a dew of blood and semen

Because our culture's geared to worship torture porn, so it seems;
Our culture's geared to worship torture porn, in any form;
Everybody likes a dose of torture porn, so they do;
Everybody loves torture porn,
(Except me).

I only came once a year –
One too many times for you.
I've seen the way you unwrap presents;
Performing autopsies on pheasants
Wouldn't strike you as so unpleasant,
Wouldn't be as difficult a thing to do.

You couldn't sing for croaking,
It was the fashion of your age.
Dead by name, dead by nature:
You were a pitifully morbid creature,
Painting Pierrotesque your features.
Opening arteries onstage –

You liked to watch the blood flow
Over your scrawny Swedish arms,
And the horror on the faces
Of the people in those places
Where you dealt in dead disgraces,
Vomited your vocal charms.

You left me a dead badger
In a wet bag, like a broken toy,
Where others would leave milk and biscuits.
I've a bucket: do you want to kick this?
Did I fuck up your winter wish-list?
I knew you had a death-wish, boy.

If you want something doing,
Do it yourself. That's what they say, right?
And although I admit it's a shame
That outside Oslo you shot out your brain,
That act was the closest you got to being sane.
I remember that one winter night,

Flying over the peninsula –
Full was the moon, high was the tide:
I was on my way to a conference in France –
I stopped to watch you chase a cat around the garden in your pants.
I caught the glint of your kitchen knife, at a second glance,
And I shook my head, and sighed.

Dead by Christmas

for PER YNGVE OHLIN

Klára

I remember that beer-soaked summer,
That pungent summer in pregnant Prague.
On scuffed grass languidly I would lounge,
Staring at the sky till it promised dark.

I made a mess in the patchy park
Behind the T-Mobile Arena,
Where disused tramlines curved and converged,
Where sweaty torsos queued for Gambrinus

Past a pissed tramp, shaking his penis
At passing punks, despite vacant loos.
A million differing breeds of dog
Paraded the paths, presented their poos,

While I sat and watched and processed booze;
A petrol-guzzling engine, sweating;
Emitting both heat and noise; eating
Hot dogs or smažak – sometimes forgetting

To eat altogether: just getting high
In bushes, collapsing on the green,
Glimpsing a fleeting feeling of joy
In the sky, and imagining I'd seen

A speck of you falling, feather-clean,
On a Bohemian-blue canvas.
By May I'd jettisoned most classes;
I'd stand and stare at statues of Jan Hus –

A cosy clangour of tram and bus
To keep me company, and a pad
And pen I'd barely used – then I'd walk
Up Wenceslas Square, barer than it had

Been on any late Sunday when bad
Lads from Kent or Fife would blight its nights,
Shed wads in its strip clubs, white-wash
Cobbles with vomit and try to start fights.

By a fast-food shack I'd scan the heights;
Trying to memorize the skyline,
I'd settle on the bank where you worked
And fantasize your name on the by-line

Of the postmodern play we'd co-write
If you weren't married to some Czech guy.
I tried to adjectivize faces
As they shot me glances and passed by,

Unaware that my intrusive eye
Rendered most such notes invalid:
See this colour brick, this make of car;
This teenager, tanned; pensioner, pallid;

This grated carrot passed for salad;
And this metrically measured beer glass.
One day I inverted a shoebox,
Spread my acrylic paints on the grass,

And killed time before taking a class
In your office. The results weren't great.
I'd prepared a lesson on grammar
But we finished over an hour late;

We browsed your holiday snaps. The date
I remember: my oldest brother
Had his picture in the NME,
And I'd recently taken another

Student on: a guy like no other,
Who owned a castle and donated
Blood and sperm on a monthly basis;
Who as a youth, for a girl, translated

Cure lyrics and was disappointed
With the results; who enthused for hours
About his many sexy conquests.
Had I but a tenth of his powers,

I daydreamed, well then I would wow her.
I'd leave swathes of lovers in my wake,
Scandal would be my shadow constant,
Lust would dictate my every mistake;

"Confessions of a Repentant Rake"
I'd call my autobiography:
It would sell by the suitecaseful, and
No one would guess the author was me

Except you, and you would choose to be
True, and discreet. In my flat, replete,
I would sit on the cigarette-burnt sofa
And watch Sex and the City on repeat

And think about you, while in the street
Outside the sounds of society
Refused to cease, even through hot nights.
I wrote poor poems and drank builders' teas

And applied for MAs, overseas.
You said you'd been redecorating
Your flat with your boyfriend for two years.
On the way home I was close to hating

Him, whom I knew not; contemplating
Later, I came close to tears, but laughed –
Taking a quick shower in the bath –
("... picking lemons with William Howard Taft ...")

Recalling what you said and just how daft:
(Or was it "... sipping consommé ..."?) that
"Toes" and "fingers" were the same in Czech.
The same word, at any rate. I mean, what

Kind of civilized race allows that?
The song stopped, I switched the player off.
I thought about Amelia Earhart –
Lit a cigarette, and began to cough –

Wondered whether, when her plane took off,
She knew she had all that in her head;
And whether if, as the song had it,
All that flashed before her, then she was dead.

I'd not forget you, I think I said;
I knew you'd cause some slight contusion.
Today I saw that book you gave me
And smiled, recalling my own confusion

When I'd just reached a conclusion
As to whether you were beautiful
And you said, "I am parachutist!"
You missed the article, as usual.

Creative destruction, said Marx,
Is the fat cat catching its tail:
Devouring like Ouroboros.
Catastrophic capital loss
Leaves impressions across the sand
As longevous as any beaching whale.

Creation, on the other hand,
Picasso famously stated,
Is destructive by its nature –
And him, famously, a painter.
But perhaps, if you focus in
On some of the brushstrokes Pablo painted,

Your best eye might make out a thin
Fault line rent asunder, or catch
The echo of an explosion.
Bringing this idea to motion,
Pinoncelli "happened" upon
A Fountain or two of the copy batch

Of eight commissioned by Duchamp
With urine twice: a hammer once.
He said it was "A great white whale,
A golden calf, a holy grail,"
But it's tethered, weathered and there.
The beret, these days a cap for a dunce,

Signifies – therefore is not – flair;
But what's on your collective head,
The public, which is what you are,
(Postmodern Op, Deco, Dada?)
Watching Yuan Chai and Jian Jun Xi
Jumping on Tracey Emin's bed?

Watching the crowd that's watching me,
I'm Michael Landy breaking down:
Each time a poem forms, I die
A little, never to retry
The title one more time. What larks!
My modus operandi is a frown.

Destroy your art

Ill of the dead

Armed with a chisel and equipped with the time
Between the burdens of age and doubts of youth,
With magical mana and the manner of a mime,
I set out under darkness, to seek my truth.

My poise was proper but my focus was flawed:
I began before my ideas were solid.
By morning I'd amassed an audience who were awed
By my work, so I shirked my chores and grew squalid

In my observance of all that was torrid;
My beard grew matted with the fruit they fed me,
My forehead sported flowers and my cheeks, hued florid,
Bore testimony to luxuries deadly.

I eschewed untruths like they asked me to do,
Completed tasks on time – and budget, to boot.
Growing wearier by the day with their treasures, I threw
Down my tools one evening and declared a moot.

We met between the roots of an immense oak;
The mayor and the cardinal, the king and I,
Observed in reverential quiet by the common folk:
I addressed them all, though I spoke to the sky.

"As long as I lived, and as long as I spoke,
 As long as grass became flat beneath my tread,
 As long as I built with every stone my chisel broke,
 I've longed to be let to speak ill of the dead;

"Ill of the men from whom we inherited
 All of the blood that now ferments in our tuns;
 Ill of the men to whom history has merited
 Statues for their sins and mansions for their sons;

"Ill of the dead man whose bust I cast this day,
 Whose first six wives were beheaded, one and all,
 To whom the suffering of others was sport and play,
 Who tripped his own servants just to watch them fall,

"And ill of my very own dear grandfather
 Who beat my own dad, who then beat me in turn;
 He might not be dead yet but, you know, I'd much rather
 The old bastard lived to see his empire burn—"

And I'd have continued my jeremiad
But that at that moment the cumuli broke:
And I felt a pain both in the brain and the backbone,
And a voice I recognized not at all spoke:

Economics

There is no argument yet made
That's not economic:
No fundament spoke sundrily,
Nor topical tonic;
No, neither is there any act –
Or even inkling
Of thought, or muscle memory –
Nor any other thing.

There is no conversation
That is truly idle:
No human breath or sign exchanged
Which is neither grooming
Nor bridal; no, nor are tears shed
Upon another's end
Excepting when the dead is thought
To be a foe or friend.

There is no true motivation
To act an isolate:
Because, to culture's brains and bits,
Economy is the gut.
And, ah, how I would borders scrub –
The freer for to be,
But freedom's price does vary so,
Depending where you be.

I would exchange my hot young blood
For your equality,
But no exchange is fair, played out
In this economy.
So much goodwill, so many gifts
I would impart for free,
But giving just breeds taking – in
Any economy.

I would that all my words were wind
And my wishes were rain,
But my intent is all I own
And my verse is in vain;
For many things I wish I knew
And had the art to show,
But I – like you – have work to do
And my fair face to show.

A red eye glints and squints,
Shedding a single brilliant tear.

A paradigmatic hatching here
Of efforts extracted across stints

Is worth a planet's held breath;
A ritual symbolizing death

And rebirth, and death again.
The worn seat that bears the newborn's weight

Is sworn to beat out the whole heart rate
By popping the cork to this new reign:

A circle of metal, cold;
A priceless work of art, framed with gold.

The crowning

Sculptures of nothing

for STEWART LEE

Substantial vultures
Stalk ailing prey
Through elephant graveyards
In the cold light of day.

Veiled intentions
Are unspoken pacts;
Aesthetic pleasures
Are unproven facts.

The senses succumbing
To an unholy haze;
Memory's spectrum
Made so many greys.

Meat in the field,
Meat in the street;
Meet in the bowels,
Meet in the peat.

Cultures of mourning
Anticipate grief
While the light of the evening
Rises beneath.

Songs of the spirit
Sung by the lungs;
Stairways to heaven,
Short a few rungs.

Answers are questions
In the ears of the young:
All of creation
Contained in one tongue.

Inklings of instance
Demanding Danegeld:
To have and to hold,
Be had, and be held.

Performing bonobos
Operate guns
At picket line borders
Under Indian suns.

Figureless shadows
Blind the best seers;
David-Tibetan
Personified fears.

Informative stories
Battle for space
With virtual debris,
Leather and lace.

A plague of knowledge
In a Trojan toad
On the hard shoulder
Of an empty road.

A salty parchment
In a mouldy cave
Begging to be bartered
To a better grave.

Uncontacted tribesmen
Throw spears at planes.
Veteran surgeons
Transplant their own brains.

Amateur masons
With excellent tools
Build structures to die for
For ungrateful fools:

Houses of sand,
Cathedrals of stone,
Castles of happenstance,
Coffins of bone.

Worms of reluctance
Digest our best hopes:
Unwritten letters
In sent envelopes.

Pragmatic dogma
Proves crime doesn't pay:
Sculptures of nothing
In marble, in clay.

Doubtless

Just a trope in your narrative,
A tincture in your soap:
Not a presence to be noticed
Without a microscope.

What's the scope of your horror or
The horror of your scope?
What's the worst you could wish for?
Do you think you could cope?

What's the word at the art school?
What's your damage? What's your dope?
Give yourself something to work with:
Give yourself enough rope,

And don't hope to be able to
Bring it to the table
If you introvert yourself to
Make yourself capable

Of composition. Compare then
He who is culpable
For fabricating a feeling
With she who fakes a fable.

There's no difference nor indifference
To me discernible;
I'd just as well now try torching
A bridge unburnable.

Birth a baby, call it Burden:
Have a child, call it Hope;
Change your own name to Sacrifice:
Ear-in-an-envelope.

Can a man who makes his fortune
Singing songs about pain
His second album to his first's
Relationship explain?

Had I the wherewithal to wear
Appropriate hats to
Any given event: all being
Well, that would doubtless do.

Mistaken for art or rubbish

My "art" is stacked against
Wrought-iron railings, painted black,
In front of the building
I've recently lived in,
Awaiting the bin men as
Bits of cardboard or hardboard,
Decorated in acrylic or collage
And as dusty as 2D objects can be:
Canvases neither canny nor uncanny.

They've followed me from flat to flat,
Even up and down a few hills,
Never having to excuse their presence;
They won't pay their way by paying bills:
Their pleasance is a time that kills,
But they fit neatly behind furniture,
Between wardrobes and walls,
Even upon walls, until one of them falls,
Awakening me at three a.m.
With the sense of a forsaken friend,
Or the forgotten gist of a to-do list.

I've come to resent them.
As much as I once loved to present them
I hate now to behold them
Unfolding from every case-unpacking.
I'm lacking the longing I once had
To provoke such exclamations as
"I never knew you were artistic!"

"Look at me," they seem to scream,
"I have so much to say!"
But that's all they've ever said.

Good art should ask questions,
Because what are answers but
Questions when they're dead?
And what is art but something you did
That nobody told you to do?
That you did just because?
That you did just for you,
And can't possibly be or mean
Anything to anyone else?

I imagine art comes from the heart.
I don't remember where they came from;
Only dates indicate their inception:
And only I can decide their fate,
So, better not never but late,

I imagine them looking down on me
From creatively named colour schemes
Watching over me in my new home,
A place I plan to be happy,
Frowning at my audacity
In pretending to be an adult.
They find the same faults with me
That I see in them,
I think.

This morning they watched me walking
To the bus stop
As far as perspective would allow.
Where are they now?
If the council will allow it
They are on their way to landfill:
Sentenced to a full stop.

For a decade I've produced one or two a year,
And they've amassed around me like a fear,
A sorry phobia of walking forwards,
Or a foreword that never
Gives way to a story.
No more.

I only hope they've been taken by someone,
Mistaken for art or rubbish,
By the time I return tonight
To unlock my front door.